BECOMING THE BOLD MISSIONARY

A POWERFUL GUIDE THAT WILL OPEN DOORS TO SUCCESS IN THE MISSION FIELD

BECOMING THE BOLD MISSIONARY

A POWERFUL GUIDE THAT WILL
OPEN DOORS TO SUCCESS
IN THE MISSION FIELD

by

George D. Durrant

BONNEVILLE BOOKS™
Springville, Utah

ISBN: 1-55517-673-9
v.1

Published by Bonneville Books
Imprint of Cedar Fort Inc.
www.cedarfort.com

Distributed by:

Typeset by Kristin Nelson
Cover design by Adam Ford
Cover design © 2002 by Lyle Mortimer

Printed in the United States of America
10 9 8 7 6 5 4 3 2 1

Printed on acid-free paper
Library of Congress Cataloging-in-Publication Data

Durrant, George D.
 Becoming the Bold Missionary : a powerful guide that will open the doors to success in the mission field / by George D. Durrant.
     p. cm.
 ISBN 1-55517-673-9 (pbk. : alk. paper)
1. Missionaries--Training of. 2. Church of Jesus Christ of Latter-Day
Saints--Missions. 3. Mormon Church--Missions. I. Title.
 BX8661 .D86 2002
 266'.9332--dc21
                                    2002006734

Dedicated to my companion, Marilyn,
who served with boldness in the British Mission.

And to all the noble sister missionaries
who teach with natural boldness.

TABLE OF CONTENTS

1

TO BE BOLD OR NOT TO BE BOLD, THAT IS THE QUESTION

A Glad Case Of Boldness

One of my favorite stories is that of Sister Franks:

A sophisticated man, after hearing Sister Franks tell of the origin of the Book of Mormon, said in a skeptical tone, "So, you claim that this man, Joseph Smith, saw an angel. The angel told him about a set of golden plates buried in a hill. You further claim that Smith went out and got those plates and translated them from an ancient language into English. Is that what you're saying?"

Sister Franks leaned forward, looked into his eyes and replied, "That is exactly what we are saying."

(The Missionary Guide)

A Sad Case Of Wishy Washy

I had just become a senior companion. We had taught a family the first two discussions and we were now returning for the third one. Our hopes were high for this young couple. To our surprise, as we entered their home, they introduced us to an uncle who was a teacher of philosophy at the local university. He was gracious but also intimidating.

I offered to leave and return again when they did not have company. The husband told us to proceed so that the uncle could also learn of our beliefs. The uncle added, "I'm very interested in your message. Please go right ahead as if I was not here."

We nervously took our seats and began the discussion. I was hesitant at first to ask if we could pray. However, knowing that I should, I ask them if a prayer would be all right. They, and the uncle, told us to please do so.

After the prayer, I reviewed our former messages about the Lord's true church which was established in the New Testament. We continued by explaining how that church was taken from the earth during the great apostasy. I carefully avoided looking in the direction of the uncle. I tried to not be to direct in my teaching and offered the ideas as my opinions and not as facts. I was hoping that by doing this I would not offend this learned man. The family responded very favorably. The uncle sat silently.

I then stated, "The story that I'm about to relate takes a lot of faith to believe. However, it seems to me to be the only way the church of Jesus Christ could be restored to the earth." Due to my nervousness, my words were coming from my head and not from my heart. I felt uncomfortable. I continued on by saying, "Before I tell you the story of Joseph Smith I want you to know that this is the incredible part. Most people don't believe this story, but in my opinion I think it really happened."

I then related the vision of the appearance of the Father and the Son.

I said, "Joseph Smith was told by the Lord that all the churches were wrong."

The philosophy professor interrupted and said, "Elder, could I break in here and ask you a question or two about what you have just said?"

He stroked his beard and in a most kind and soft voice said, "If I understand you correctly, you said that God said that all the other churches were wrong. Do you really think a just God would say that?"

I replied, "He didn't say the people were bad in the other churches or that they are wrong. He just said that their doctrine is false. Besides, in my opinion there can only be one true church. If our church is true, and the other churches are different in doctrine, then they cannot be completely true."

"Don't you feel it a bit presumptuous to say one church is true? That means that you feel that the billions of people who are Buddhist or Hindus or members of other Christian Churches all have false beliefs. Surely you can't believe that."

"I didn't say that. I just said that in my opinion someone has to be right. And I think that is our church. I guess that others think that they are right. Besides as one wise man said, 'You have to stand for something or you will fall for anything.'"

The professor smiled, shook his head in disbelief and said, "The statement you just quoted does not make any sense at all."

"Well, even if our church is not the only true one, it is still the best way of life that there is."

The professor smiled and said, "I'm afraid that I have offended you. Please go ahead and complete your message. I'll just listen and not make any more comments."

I weakly replied, "You didn't offend us. Anyway we have said what we came to say and we need to get going to another appointment."

As we were leaving I turned to the husband and said, "We will come back next Wednesday night if that will be all right."

He replied, "I don't think we want to go any further with this. We have loved having you come, but I'm sure others will be more receptive to what you have to teach."

Disappointedly I replied, "Okay, if that is how you feel. Anyway, maybe we will see you again sometime."

As we rode away on our tandem bicycle, I said to Elder Blair, "What did you think of that?"

It caused me great pain as he replied, "Don't you think that you were a little wishy washy?"

The Choice Is Yours

Many changes will take place within you as you serve your mission. The most needed change of all will be to move away from the fears that make you wishy washy and toward the virtues which will make you bold.

The message of this book will help you be bold. Just as Sister Franks, you will boldly respond to both the learned and the simple:

"Are you saying that Jesus Christ is the Son of God and the Savior of the world?"

"That is exactly what we are saying."

"Are you saying Joseph Smith saw Heavenly Father and Jesus Christ?"

"That is exactly what we're saying."

"Are you saying the Book of Mormon is the word of God?"

"That is exactly what we're saying."

"Are you saying the Church of Jesus Christ of Latter-day Saints is the only true and living church upon the earth?"

"That is exactly what we're saying."

"So you are saying, 'I will be a bold missionary.'"

"That is exactly what I'm saying."

2

BEING A BOLD MISSIONARY

My companion, Elder McInnis was a bold missionary. His manners were meticulous. He had the bearing of a king and the graciousness of a secretary of state. Yet, he was as common as only someone form Eagar, Arizona could be. As we taught, he was fearless in asking the people to live a Christ-like life. His boldness in inviting them to come to church, to give up drinking tea, to pay tithing, and to be baptized shocked me. As we taught the people, I'd think, "Don't push them so hard, Elder McInnis." It seemed to me that every time, just as we were beginning to feel the Spirit of the Lord, he'd spoil everything by challenging them to kneel with us in prayer. Then he would ask one of them to lead the prayer. I'd be shocked and relieved when they'd say, "Yes, we'll do it." I'd want to shout, "Way to go! Elder McInnis, way to go!" The people liked and trusted him because of his loving boldness.

Great missionaries are bold. You will be a bold missionary. This book will help you to be bold.

Not All Missionaries Have Equal Amounts Of The Personal Ingredients Needed To Be Bold

We all take different baggage with us on our mission. Some baggage is positive and some is negative. Elder McInnis packed different baggage than I did.

I wasn't there in Eagar, Arizona when Elder McInnis packed his stuff. He must have needed a lot of room in his suitcases to pack all the facets of his natural and spontaneous personality, all his charm, all his confidence, and all the grand qualities he had accumulated in high school and college.

A month later it was my time to pack. I did not need much room for my confidence. I did not have much of that. I should have gained confidence while I was in school. However, that is where I'd somehow lost it. I lost part of it in the gymnasium. I lost another part in the lunchroom, and I lost a lot of it in the halls of the school and at the dances. Confidence is sort of invisible and once it wanders away, it sure is hard to find again. So I packed my extra navy blue suit in the part of my suitcase where confidence should have gone.

In those days, the way I looked in navy blue with my white shirt and tie was the closest thing I could come to genuine confidence. I didn't need much room in my suitcase for my charm, nor my personality. I only had a meager amount of each of those.

When Elder McInnis arrived in England his trunk was nearly bursting open, and its contents filled him inside and outside with the attributes of a successful missionary.

A month later when I arrived and opened my trunk, there was not much personality there. However I sensed that there was something there that I couldn't remember packing. It was a big bundle of desire, surrounded with a good supply of hope. With all my heart I wanted to be a good missionary. I longed to be bold enough to assist

8

someone to join the Church. I was a bit doubtful of that happening, because in the past, I didn't even have enough persuasive powers to convince a girl to accompany me on a date.

The negative baggage, which some Elders bring with them to their missions, includes the emotional and spiritual scars of the past. Scars that may have come because of poor academic achievements, irresponsible behaviors, frustrations in athletics or other endeavors, unfulfilled desires to achieve popularity, lack of confidence and self-esteem, and little self discipline.

If such negative baggage fills your suitcase, remember that such inadequacies need not stop you from being a bold missionary. Your vision and desire for the future can and will be more powerful than the restraint of your lack-luster past.

On the other hand, perhaps you, in your pre-mission days have been accorded many opportunities and have gained frequent successes. Maybe you, in your past, have acquired pleasing social skills, developed spiritual awareness, gained sound organizational ability, and have many other ingredients of greatness.

If such positive baggage fills your suitcase, be aware that from such a foundation, you can, if filled with intense desire, serve an extraordinary mission. You can also help many other missionaries to do the same. You should be aware that one missionary can change a whole mission. I've seen bold missionaries do that. Why not you?

All Missionaries Have Equal Opportunities To Become Bold

The great equalizer between missionaries who seem unequal in the beginning, is the intensity of each one's hope and desire to be a bold messenger of the truth. The desire to nurture the seeds of boldness which are within him, and the hope that each has to have a glorious mission are the greatest predictors of a missionary success.

Remember:

- Be you an extrovert or an introvert, you can be bold.

- Be you a high school big wheel or a high school dud, you can be bold.

- Be you a quick learner or a slow learner, tough guy or wimp, social butterfly or wall flower, extraordinary or ordinary, impressive or unimpressive, confident or fearful, on your mission you can and will be bold.

The seeds of boldness are within you. On your mission, nourish those seeds and you will be bold.

3

WHAT IT MEANS TO BE BOLD

I'll say more about Elder McInnis later, but for now let's skip ahead to my next companion, Elder Blair. This amazing Elder was youngest of seventeen children and was raised in Shelley, Idaho. When he first arrived in England, he and I worked together. I recall this experience:

Elder Blair and I rode the tandem bike to the street meeting spot. This was to be his first opportunity at such an activity.

I gave my speech on the fact that the true church in the New Testament had apostles. I pointed out that the true church today should also have apostles. I reasoned the same way on revelation. I pointed out that there could only be one true church, and if another church was different than the true church then that church could not be true. It was a very good talk even if I do say so myself.

I was sure that Elder Blair would be impressed. I walked over to him and said. "It is your turn. Try to give a talk something like I just gave." I then asked, "Seeing as this is your first time to do this, do you need me to give you a few ideas?"

He quickly replied. "I do not need your help. My mother told me what to say before I left home." He then took his position and shouted, "My friends of Hull, I'm here to tell you to repent." Then there was a long silence. He said no more. After a time he walked over to where I was.

I said, "Is that it?"

He replied, "That is it. My mother said my message was to say nothing more than repentance, and I did that. So let's go."

I thought at the time that my talk had surely been better than Elder Blair's had been. Now, after all these years, I'm no longer sure of that. Bold missionaries are the ones who cry repentance to the people. Of course they elaborate on it a bit more than Elder Blair did that day. If they had not done so, the Book of Mormon and the other scriptures would be a bit shorter than they are.

As we rode away on the tandem bike, Elder Blair peddled a bit harder than usual.

As time passed, I learned that he was the most pure-hearted man that I have ever known. He was not the most sophisticated of the missionaries. He was, on the other hand, the most virtuous. In his humble, sweet way Elder Blair was bold. When he gave a talk in a church meeting, he would spend his first thirty seconds at the pulpit by just standing there smiling at the people. Then, while he continued to smile, he would tell them of the things of which they needed to repent. The people loved to be called to repentance by Elder Blair. Not only did he do what his mother told him to do, but he also did what the Lord told him to do. He was bold.

Now before we go on, please say out loud the word, "bold."
Here you go, **"Bold!"**

That was all right, but now say it with more boldness.
Ready, **"Bold!!"**

That was better. Now really be bold and say it again. Go for
it, **"Bold!!!"**

Spiritual Boldness

If you increased the volume of your voice each time you
said the word, "bold," you could miss the point of this book.
Added volume in your voice, or added zest in your personality
is not the kind of "bold" we are striving for. Brazen recklessness
and abandon in your behavior is not the meaning of the "bold"
that you will seek on your mission. Those qualities are all right,
but they are not the quality that we are seeking. The "bold" we
are talking about is not the dictionary definition of bold. We
seek to be "spiritually bold."

The "bold" we are talking about is not "self-confidence." It
is "Christ-confidence."

The "bold" that we are seeking is not characterized by an
attitude that would cause some to make these statements:

I love to get up in front of a crowd and perform.
I feel real confident in every social situation.
I'll be the head of a company by age thirty.
I'm willing to risk it even though it sounds impossible.
Nothing scares me.

I'm sure you would like to have such confidence. I know

that I would. However that is not the "bold" that will make you a great missionary.

Neither is the boldness we are seeking the tactic of using your testimony as if it was a six-shooter for settling religious differences by saying:

> "You think your church is right, but I know that mine is the true church. So there (*bang, bang, bang*) take that."

Instead your boldness will be to feel the promptings of the Holy Spirit and then express yourself in this manner:

> Mr. and Mrs. Larsen, I sense by the Spirit of the Lord that you are sincerely seeking the truth. I promise you, in the name of the Lord, that as you read the Book of Mormon and pray about it, you will know that this book is the Word of God.

The boldness that you will have is not, "Look at me" boldness. Instead it is, "Look to the Savior" boldness. It is not, "Trust me," boldness. It is, "Trust Him," boldness.

Your boldness will come because, "Your confidence (will) wax strong in the presence of God." When you feel His Spirit, you will know that you are in His presence, and you will confidently and boldly speak His words in His name.

Such boldness will come to you as you "...let virtue garnish your thoughts unceasingly." This will bring into your soul a quiet and non-compromising confidence. You will know that the Lord will back you up when you declare His truths in meekness.

With spiritual boldness you will quietly say things such as:

Brother and Sister Larsen, we can feel the spirit of the Lord as we talk with you about these sacred truths. We feel a great love for you. We know that the Lord loves you. The Lord has promised, in the Book of Malachi, that you will be able to pay your tithing. And as you do, you will also have enough money to pay all of your other bills. We promise you that through your faith in living this sacred law, you will be blessed.

Will you begin this week to pay your tithing?

"Bold" is a great word. No other word sounds so bold as does the word, "Bold." No other words pays higher tribute to a missionary than to say of him, "He is bold!"

Now say the word bold again. **"Bold!"**

That was good, but now think of this word's spiritual meaning. Don't say it louder, instead say it with more sincerity. Ready, **"Bold!!"**

Very good. Now really be bold and say it again as if you desired to have this quality with all our heart. Go ahead, **"Bold!!!"**

Just right.

Public Boldness Is Good, But Private Boldness Is Great

Let's skip ahead again, further into my mission, and then we will come back to Elder McInnis and Elder Blair. Elder Stephen Covey was the assistant to the president in my mission. He was the boldest man I had ever known. He and his companion, Elder Otteson, would travel all over the mission and encourage all missionaries to be bold.

Elder Covey and Elder Otteson came to Hull to speak to the missionaries serving there. They told us of some of the bold things that other missionaries were doing in the mission. They recounted personal experiences about how, when on buses or on street corners they spoke up and delivered gospel messages. The more they talked the more excited I became about being more bold.

That evening these two dynamic missionaries stayed with us. Elder Otteson teamed up with my companion and Elder Covey with me. Off we went to do missionary work. I told Elder Covey that we wouldn't find very many people at home because it was Saturday night, and all the people would be at the movies. He suggested, "Well, if they're down at the movie house, why don't we go there and speak to them on the streets as they go to the movie and as they come out?"

That was a new idea to me. I could not see how that would work, but I offered no resistance. Elder Covey had a car and so we drove to a movie theater. When we arrived there about 200 people were lined up and waiting to enter the theater. Seeing this captive audience, Elder Covey rubbed his hands together with enthusiasm, smile broadly and said, "Let's go talk to those people."

I replied, "We can't do that."

"Why not?" he asked in surprise.

"Well, those people would have to listen. If they go anywhere, they will lose their place in line."

He replied, "That's the idea." He started walking toward them. As we grew closer, he turned to me and said, "Elder Durrant, it was your idea to come down here. I've never done this before, so you speak first and show me how it's done and then I'll speak." His words left me limp. I knew I couldn't just walk up there and start to speak. I also knew that I had to.

The people were lined up against the wall of the theater on the inside edge of the sidewalk. I took a position on the opposite edge, my heels up against the curb and gutter. I was as far away from them as I could get and that was about five feet. In a panic, I removed my hat, held it in left hand, stood on one foot and then the other. A few people noticed me and wondered what I was up to. I had no idea what to say. I opened my mouth and with a shaky voice began to speak, "My friends of Hull, I'm Elder Durrant and I'm a Mormon."

About thirty of the closest people ceased their private conversations. Their attention was focused directly on me. After uttering that first sentence, my panic started to lessen, and I continued, "Many of you might think us Mormons have many wives." I paused and added with a smile, "I'm a Mormon and I don't have a wife at all." They didn't smile, but I could tell they were thinking, "We can understand that."

Now I felt more relaxed and excited. I felt a surge of boldness going up and down my spine. I continued,

"Mormons don't practice polygamy in these times. I'd like to tell you what Mormons do believe. In the year 1820, a young man named Joseph Smith went out into a sacred grove of trees and he asked God which church was true. In response to his prayer, he saw God, Our Heavenly Father, and His Son, Jesus Christ."

I went on to tell those people the story of Joseph Smith and the first vision. All the while I was talking, there was one large man who had his eyes fixed right on me. He was as tall as I am and even huskier, if you can imagine that. His large size and his intent expression caused me to feel uneasy. I'd sweep my eyes from one person to another. Each one looked, at least slightly pleasant, except for this man. He looked deeply disturbed by my words. I felt that when I finished speaking, this man would actually come out of the line and attack me. I spoke a bit longer than I had intended.

When I stopped, just as I had supposed, he came out of the line straight at me. I couldn't back up because of the gutter behind me. I braced myself for his assault. As I was expecting the worst, he stopped, smiled and extended his hand in a firm handshake. Then he said, "I have never seen anyone with the courage you have." He continued, "I'd give anything to know God as you do. I wish I had the courage to do what you just did." He then thanked me for my words and my example.

Wow!!! Was I bold or what? Oh sure, what I did is one kind of boldness. However it is not the most important kind of boldness.

I found that having occasional and public boldness by doing such things as speaking to people in movie lines was easier than having "everyday boldness" on each door-step or when teaching a family in the privacy of their home. In the days that followed Elder Covey's visit, Elder Rasmussen and I were in our area going from house to house. Now, the true test of boldness would come. We now needed to approach each door with the same zest that I felt in the movie line. True boldness is not a one-time public act of bravado. Instead it is a continual attitude of speaking boldly the words of the Lord in thousands of almost private circumstances and teaching situations.

4

THE KEY TO BOLDNESS

The Lord wants his gospel to be taken to the whole world. To allow us to effectively help Him, He has given us a sacred gift. This gift is the key that unlocks the door to spiritual communication. He explains this holy process in this way:

> "...lift up your voices unto this people; speak the thoughts that I shall put into your hearts, and you shall not be confounded before men;
>
> "For it shall be given you in the very hour, yea, in the very moment, what ye shall say.
>
> "But a commandment I give unto you, that ye shall declare whatsoever thing ye declare in my name, in solemnity of heart, in the spirit of meekness in all things.
>
> "And I give unto you this promise, that inasmuch as ye do this the Holy Ghost will be shed forth in bearing record unto all things whatsoever ye shall say."
>
> *(D&C 100:5-8)*

The faith to "lift up your voice" is the Lord's invitation to you to be bold.

Then He gives you a promise that He will put into your heart, at the very moment you need to know, the thoughts that He desires you to say.

21

He adds to that promise:

"And inasmuch as we (you) do this, the Holy Ghost shall be shed forth in bearing record unto all things whatsoever ye shall say."

Then He commands you to use this sacred principle of communication, "with solemnity of heart and a spirit of meekness." Such solemnity of heart will only come when you have an intense desire to be worthy to speak for the Lord. Meekness will come as you sense that the power you have in your words is not a power within you, but rather it is a power which God sends through you.

I really don't know of anything quite so sacred, as having the Lord put a thought in your heart, having it come out in your words, and having the Holy Ghost rush in and tell people that what you just said is true. When you follow this principle of spiritual communication, your words, though not loud, will be genuine, sincere and powerful.

Let's now act as though you and I are teaching a young couple. You are my companion, and as you are speaking, a gentle thought comes into your heart. You feel a feeling which says to you, "Tell these people that you love them." You follow that prompting by saying, "Mr. and Mrs. Jamison, my companion and I feel a great love for you." Because this thought was put in your heart by the Lord, and then you spoke the words which express the thought, sent by the Holy Ghost, the people will know that we truly do love them.

You feel other impressions in your heart, so you say, "We

consider it a great honor to be in your home. We feel the spirit of love and kindness here. Some day we want to have these same feelings in our homes. We know you folks love the Lord. You know the priesthood of our Heavenly Father has been restored to the earth, and is found only in the Church of Jesus Christ of Latter-day Saints."

The couple listens intently. Inside their souls, the Holy Ghost quietly confirms to them that what they have just heard is true. The feeling them comes into your heart, "Invite them to be baptized next Saturday."

You say, "Brother and Sister Jamison I feel impressed to tell you that baptism is essential to your salvation. Because of that, Jesus Christ wants you to take upon yourselves His name and become members of His Church by being baptized. We are going to have a baptism next Saturday at three o'clock. Will you be baptized at that time?"

The Jamisons know by the power of the Holy Ghost that they should be baptized and they agree to do so.

As we speak when moved upon by the Holy Ghost, our words, "shall be the mind of the Lord, shall be the word of the Lord, shall be the voice of the Lord, and the power of God unto salvation." Salvation—our words will help people gain salvation.

Alma told his son Shiblon, "Use boldness but not overbearance..." The difference between being bold or overbearing is that when you have the Spirit, you are bold. If you're just trying to do it on your own, you're overbearing. It's as simple as that.

5

A MISSION IS THE PERFECT OPPORTUNITY TO BECOME BOLD

If you feel that you have been a bit "wishy washy" and quite lacking in boldness in your past, your mission will be the perfect time and place to change that.

A New Beginning

When you arrive on your mission you will be in a new place with new people and doing a new thing. It is a perfect place to nurture the bold seeds that are within you.

Many years ago, when I was a freshman at BYU, I first came to know a fellow classmate named Murray McInnis.

Murray was part of the "in" crowd and the girls swarmed around him. He knew how to talk with them and dance with them and laugh with them. He was always smiling and he had a seemingly fearless personality. He was the way I wanted to be, and because I wasn't the way I wanted to be, I resented him. I carefully avoided being overly friendly with him because I was sure he was not my kind of guy. Unbeknown to me, two months before I was to leave for my mission in England, Murray McInnis arrived in that same mission.

I soon also arrived there. After two days of training in London I had an interview with my mission president,

A. Hamer Reiser. As we sat together, I sensed that he did not know of my past failures. He looked at me for several seconds and although he did not say so, I could tell that he thought that I was all right—maybe even more than all right. Finally after sizing me up, he said to me, "Elder Durrant, you go to Hull."

I was shocked and asked, "Where?"

He replied, "Hull." He then spelled it for me—HULL. An hour later I was on a northbound train headed for Hull. As I rode along through the beautiful English countryside I was filled with fear. No one in Hull had ever seen me before, nor I them. Then it occurred to me that perhaps the people in Hull would think I had been all-state, maybe even student body president and hopefully that I had been immensely popular. If they thought those things, I vowed to never set them straight. Hull would be a place for new beginnings—a place where my hoped for vision of the future would be greater than the baggage of my past.

On Your Mission, Choose A Bold Missionary To Be Your Hero And Be Like Him

Two days later, I attended my first district missionary meeting. The two Elders from North Hull were a few minutes late. Hearing someone come in the back of the chapel, I turned. I was shocked to see a most familiar face. It was none other than Elder Murray McInnis, my old classmate from BYU. As he approached me, he smiled broadly and with much warmth in his voice, said, "Hello, Elder Durrant. I'm glad you're in the district." He then startled me by saying, "I remember seeing a lot of you at BYU. You impressed me there."

I stammered and by the time I was ready to respond our District Leader called us to order and we began the meeting. I couldn't fully focus on what was going on because of the feelings I'd had in seeing Elder McInnis. His warm greeting and his expression about his feelings toward me, had in an instant, changed all my past, unjustifiable feelings toward him, and had replaced them with feelings of love.

That day, I was impressed with the way Elder McInnis smiled, the way he talked, the way he taught, the way he loved. Now instead of being envious of his attributes, I was admiring him and was longing to be like him.

A few weeks later, I was elated when I was told that I was to be the junior companion to my new hero. I know there have been other missionary companionships who have been dynamic—Alma and Amulek, Paul and Barnabas—but never, according to my memory, have there been two missionaries as dynamic as Elder Murray McInnis and me, Elder George Durrant. We rode a bicycle built for two. It was called a tandem. It was a classic bit of machinery. Elder McInnis sat up in the front, and I brought up the rear. He steered and I followed. I didn't mind. I loved following him—his constant good mood and his genuine love for me and everyone, plus his confidence and friendliness made him easy to follow.

We wore hats in those days. I wish you could have seen them. They were sort of round on top. They had a narrow brim. As the English would say, we made a right smart looking pair of blokes as we cycled down the cobblestone streets of Hull. Elder McInnis had a distinctive look about him. He looked a lot like Billy Graham. Billy Graham, at that time, was not too much older than us. He was immensely popular. Many people were shocked when they first came to their door and opened it, and they thought Billy Graham was standing on their doorstep.

As time went by, I watched every move Elder McInnis made and listened to every word he spoke. Even now, more than forty years later, I can still see him standing there with his hat in his hand talking to a person who had just come to the door. "Good morning," he'd say warmly. His wide grin would cause even the most disturbed to have a difficult time to keep from smiling back. His natural, spontaneous, genuine love would get us in nearly every heart and in almost every door. I also observed that as the days passed he was adding something to his charm and warmth. He was becoming more and more bold.

Oh, how I desired to be like him. I tried to do so, but boldness did not come as easily to me as it did to him. I tried to speak as he did and smile as he did. I often wondered, as we peddled the old tandem bike, him on the front leading the way and me in the rear following perfectly, if I could ever be like him. At the same time I began to realize that there was a seed of boldness within me. Little by little I began to nourish that seed. In so doing I began unlocking the part of myself that had long been imprisoned. I was coming out of myself and feeling more like my wonderful companion. Soon, I too could get people to smile and invite us to come in. Once inside, while I was warming up as to what to say, Elder McInnis would be complimenting them on their beautiful children, the pictures on their walls, asking them, "Who decorated this house? It's beautiful."

The people loved him, and because I was trying to be like him, they liked me too.

Those were golden days for me. I was becoming what I'd always longed to be. As I write about those experiences, I am near tears of joy that there was once a time like that. In my memory, I'm once again with Elder Murray McInnis. We're in a house in England winning the trust of a family, loving them and helping them feel the Spirit, helping them resolve their concerns and boldly inviting them to be baptized. Those were golden days for me because as we challenged others to do those things that would enable them to find out for themselves that the things we taught were true, I too did those same things. I too came to know with certainty that our message was God's message. For the first time in my life, I was becoming bold. I was in a place where no one knew me as being a timid one. and I was with a man who modeled for me what I could be if I'd but be bold.

A Mission Is A Time To Form A Partnership With The Lord

Then one day, a very sad day, a letter came from the Mission Office in London. The next day Elder McInnis was to be transferred to New Castle. I was now to be senior companion to Elder Kenneth Blair.

The next morning Elder McInnis and I rode the tandem together for the last time. At the train station, I said, "Elder McInnis, I don't know what I'm going to do without you." Tears filled his eyes and mine.

"You'll do great," he said, "You'll do great."

"You'll be the best man at my wedding," I said, in an effort to let him know just how deeply I respected him.

A few minutes later, we said the most difficult goodbye that I had ever said. Never had I felt so desperate for strength beyond my own. He boarded the train, and I watched as he leaned from the window for a last goodbye, and then Elder McInnis was gone. Emptiness is the only word that comes close to describing how I felt.

An hour later, Elder Blair arrived at the train station. As the two of us walked out of the station, neither of us spoke. We pulled the tandem bicycle from the brick wall against which we had left it leaning. I swung my leg over the unfamiliar front seat and Elder Blair climbed on behind. As we headed up the road, everything looked frighteningly different from the front. Now there was so much to watch out for, I felt so desperate for direction. I knew then that sometimes being bold is nothing more than the power to keep going.

The day I moved from the back seat to the front seat of the old tandem, I learned more powerfully than ever before, that if invited, there is a third companion who will sit on a seat just in front of the front seat. This companion only rides with us, or walks with us, if we desire Him to do so. If we ask Him, He will take His seat and off we'll go. He will tell us where to turn. If the hill we're going up is steep, He will help us make it to the top. If the weather is warm and humid, He will help us still get through it. If it's cold and penetrating, He will give us inward warmth. If the people reject us, He will be the most hurt. This companion will never be transferred, and if we desire Him to do so, He will be with us always and we'll never be alone. With Him up front we will feel bold for we will know that He will tell us what to say, and he will back us up in every way.

He will go before us by sending the Holy Ghost to be our constant companion. Through the influence of the Holy Ghost, we will feel the reality of Jesus Christ. We will feel His love, His comfort, and His direction. By following the whisperings of the Holy Ghost, we will know the will of the Lord. When we follow such promptings we can boldly teach truths, extend challenges and make promises in the name of Jesus Christ. Knowing these things is the very key to being spiritually bold.

On Your Mission You Become The Lord's Agent: The Perfect Opportunity To Be Bold

Knowing that you have the right to speak in the name of Jesus Christ—to be His agent—gives you the opportunity to be bold. This pre-mission story illustrates the confidence that comes in filling the role of an agent.

There was a girl who I liked so much that I did not dare talk to her. She sat right in front of me in my history class. Every day as I walked to school I would think of clever things to say to her that day. However, when we were in class my courage failed and I said nothing.

One day my big, athletic, handsome friend, who sat two rows over, sent me a note. It read, "Ask Louise if she will go to the movie with me Friday night."

With the note in hand, I boldly tapped her on the shoulder. She turned around. I smiled a charming smile and boldly asked, "What are you doing Friday night?"

She replied, "Nothing."

"How would you like to go to the movie?" I asked.

She replied, "I'd love to."

"All right, Don over there wants to take you."

What made the difference that day? Why did my fears depart and allow courage to take over? I became Don's agent. When I was speaking for another, it gave me the courage to be bold.

The greatest discovery I made while on my mission was the fact that I did not speak for myself. I spoke for the Lord. Figuratively speaking, I had a note from Him which said. "Ask people to repent and be baptized. Do it in my name." With such a charge from Him, I became His agent. I proclaimed the gospel in His name, and that allowed me to be bold.

6

VIRTUE IS THE FOUNDATION OF BOLDNESS

Wanting, Longing, And Trying With All Your Heart To Be Virtuous Is The Key To Boldness

It is not possible to be perfectly virtuous at all times, but it is possible to want to be. It is in wanting to be virtuous that your power to be bold will come.

Elder Blair was the most virtuous of the missionaries. He truly tried to be like the Savior.

Oh, he was not always the epitome of virtue. There were times when we did not get along perfectly. At the time, I was certain that it was his fault. Once while we were tracting, we got in an argument over a song we heard some Baptist ladies singing. I was sure they were singing, "Bringing in the sheep."

Elder Blair told me that I was wrong. He said that the words were, "Bringing in the sheaves."

After arguing for a few minutes, I disgustedly decided that there was no way to convince him of his error. We developed a bit of ill will toward each other and so we returned to where we had parked the tandem and headed home. We did not speak to each other all the way home. I could see little virtue in Elder Blair on that day, nor he in me.

So we see that even Elder Blair struggled to maintain constant and perfect virtue. Later I learned that he was right about the song, but, in my opinion, he was wrong to insist that he was right.

Listening To The Enticings Of The Holy Spirit Will Lead You Ever Closer To Virtue

King Benjamin told us that life *naturally* has a downward pull. He told us the way to counter this drag was to yield... "to the enticings of the Holy Spirit..."

The words "yield" and "enticings" are gentle and inviting words.

Yielding to the Lord's enticings will enable you to step off from life's natural and downward escalator and step on to God's spiritual and upward escalator. In doing so, we can become "... submissive, meek, humble, patient, full of love..." We can be virtuous.

Yielding to the enticings of the Holy Spirit provides the foundation for boldness.

Boldness Comes As You Yield Your Will To The Lord's Will

Picture in your mind two separate paths that cross each other like a big X. Christ is walking down one of the path and you are walking down the other one. You see a sign which says, "yield." You yield and let Him go first. Then you come in just slightly behind Him. That way you can see where's He's going, and you can go there, too. You can hear His voice and say what

He says. You can see how He treats people, and you treat them that way. You can hear the enticings of the Holy Spirit, and yield, your will to His. Then you will be bold.

Alma said, *"And now I would that ye should be humble, and be submissive and gentle; and easy to be entreated..."*

Missionaries who are easy to be entreated gain the power to be bold. When your mission president and other mission leaders speak, follow their counsel. When through prayer or in scripture study, you find inspiration, follow it. When you are teaching and you feel the promptings of the Holy Spirit open your mouth and speak the thoughts of your heart. Be easy to be entreated and you will have the power to be bold.

Past And Present Failures At Seeking To Be Virtuous, Can Motivate You To Do Better

Most missionaries struggle in their attempts to feel constantly virtuous and constantly bold. Falling short of what we desire to be can lead to discouragement. This is the reason our mission time is often the most difficult time of our lives. When hard times come prayer is the foundation of recovery. The only prayer that is always answered is the prayer for strength.

I remember an Elder Smith in Tennessee. His mission years were difficult for him. As he came to me for his appointed interview he was downcast. His health was not good. He had labored for some eighteen months without great success. His desires to be a leader were not being realized. He had come to the end of his rope. He did not wish to go home, but looking ahead he felt that he just could not endure another six months. As he told me these things, both he and I shed tears. I had no great advice for him. I stood, walked behind him, and laid my hands on his head and gave him a blessing. It was mainly a blessing to tell him how much the Lord loved him and appreciated all that he had down. It was an appeal for strength. It was a promise that, as he hung on, things would get better. We embraced and he went out into the cold. I could not go with him, but the Lord could and did.

Six moths later he came to his final departure meeting at the mission home. His last six months had not been spectacular. But his spirit was. He was filled with boldness as he proclaimed how much the Lord had blessed him. He was ready for all the remaining chapters of his life.

Being virtuous is not so much an end as it is a journey. The process of gaining virtue is not a sprint-it is a marathon and longer. You don't have to run faster than you have strength or run with perfect form. However you need to stay on the track. Some days you'll glide right along. Other days you will hit the wall. Keep running the race with a willing heart. Then in those sacred moments of your work, you will feel the Spirit of the Lord. You will be bold in teaching the truth to those you love. You will challenge them to do the Lord's will. You will promise them blessing in the name of Jesus Christ. As you do these things for others, great blessings of encouragement will come to you.

7

BOLDNESS COMES AS YOU CHANGE WEAKNESSES INTO STRENGTHS

Bold Missionaries Stay The Same, And Yet They Become Different

When I was called on my mission I went to the missionary training home in Salt Lake City. My first companion there was Elder Mahlon Edwards from Boulder City, Nevada. Our personalities and natures seemed to be on the same frequency. We could talk to one another about our deepest thoughts and concerns. On the third and last day of our training we walked to a place called Heinz Apothecary. There we purchased some Dramamine pills to take during our upcoming voyage to England. (We had been told that if we took these pills we wouldn't get seasick on the way to England. We later found that wasn't true.) As we walked several blocks together we had a very meaningful conversation which was filled with some seriousness and quite a lot of humor.

When we were nearly back to the mission home, Elder Edwards said something I've never forgotten. He said, "Elder Durrant, I'm glad we've become friends. I really like being around you. I like your sense of humor and your personality." He then added, "Promise me that while you're on your mission you won't change."

Now, as I look back on my mission, I feel that I really didn't change while I served in England. When I came home, I was the same George Durrant. Yet at the same, time I was really a "new" George Durrant. I hope that I was the same in the ways that Elder Edwards had admired, but I believe I was different in the ways that the Lord admired.

Perhaps in some ways you do not want to change while you serve your mission. You don't want to lose any of your hair, your athletic prowess, nor your fun loving nature. You hope that when you return you will still have the same feelings toward your good friends as you have now and that you will be able to hang out with them in the same fun loving manner that you now enjoy. You don't want to become self-righteous, but you desire to be righteous.

When you return home you will be the same person that your friends and your family love. Your pre-mission associates will still know you and they will still love you. You'll still have the same personality. You will still enjoy many of the things you formerly enjoyed. However, when you return home, because you have been bold, you will be different. Your boldness will have made you different in many ways that really matter.

Changing Weaknesses Into Strengths
Brings Boldness

If we took a poll on the scriptures missionaries love the most, Ether 12:27 would be near the top. There, Mormon tells us:

"And if (missionaries) come unto me I will show unto them their weakness. I give unto (missionaries) weakness that they may be humble; and my grace is sufficient for all (missionaries) that humble themselves before me; for if (missionaries) humble themselves before me, and have faith in me, then will I make weak things become strong unto them."

We can change our personal weaknesses into our personal strengths. That is one of the greatest principles that has ever been known. That is at the heart of religion. That is the heart of the atonement of Christ—his grace—which makes it possible for us to change.

This message is one of pure hope. It is the key to your entire future. The Lord promises you that as you humble yourself, listen to the enticings of the Holy Spirit, and become easy to be entreated, your weaknesses, through your partnership with Jesus Christ, can become your strength.

How does that happen? For you and for me the specifics of this promise will be different because we each have different weaknesses. However, the process for each of us will work in the same wonderful manner.

From The Weakness Of Feeling Inadequate To The Strength Of Feeling Capable

In my case here are some specifics:

In high school I wanted to be a star basketball player, but it's difficult to be a star from the bench. I wanted to be student-body president, but I was never nominated. I wanted to be popular but the girls in my school were dumb and so I went largely unnoticed.

Whenever I'd try to go down the freeway of life, Heavenly Father would say, "No, George you go down the back roads."

I developed a feeling of inferiority. These feelings created a weakness within me that kept me from doing and being many things that I could have done or been. These feeling of inferiority were part of the baggage I took with me on my mission.

While I served as a missionary, I learned that in the name of Jesus Christ and by His Grace, I could do things that I had never before imagined. I found that although I could not rid myself of feelings of inferiority, I could declare my independence from such feelings. I could act as though I did not have such inward concerns. I began reaching out to others instead of always looking into my own self. I began acting and feeling in ways that I had never done before. At the time I was making these changes, I could still recall sitting on the bench during a basketball game and longing to be the star. With that and other "back-road memories," I could, with understanding and empathy, invite others who suffered from my ailment to stand up and get in the game of life. If they said, "What do you care? Why do you want me to change?"

I could say, "Because I understand and because I've changed and because I want you to change. I love you. Now get up and get in the game."

Thus my weakness, my inferiority complex, became a strength in enabling me to understand, love and help others.

Changing From The Weakness Of Self-control To The Strength Of Self-mastery

As mission presidents interview missionaries they talk together about how the work can be advanced in the best manner. They discuss the personal welfare of the missionary. Sometimes the missionary, in his desire to fully repent, tells the president of some of his personal weaknesses—weaknesses which have led to indiscretions and compromises of mission rules and the moral code. The missionary who wants to be worthy feels saddened that he is not able to bring his behaviors into compliance with his righteous desires. He feels he is weak and has little character or integrity.

For example, a missionary desires to get out of bed on time each day. He pledges to the president and to himself that he will do so. He does so for several mornings and then he falters and sleeps in. He regrets this, but seems incapable of overcoming this weakness. In his next interview with the president he feels guilty and decides that if he is asked about this, he will be untruthful. He feels relieved when the president does not ask him specifically about this matter.

Soon sleeping-in is a habit. He feels discouraged. His scripture study time is gone. He senses that he has little power as a person or as a teacher. He feels timid and insecure. He feels little self worth.

He feels desperation as he considers his ways. Then he, like the prodigal son, comes to himself. He listens to the enticings of the Holy Spirit. The next morning he gets up on time. He writes a letter to the mission president. In which he says:

> "President, I sleep in, but I don't want to. I didn't come out here to sleep in. It's hard for me to get up, but I did it this morning and I'll do it from now on. Would you write down that I'm going to get up on time and the next time you see me, the first question I want you to ask me is, 'Are you getting up on time?' And I'll tell you the truth. The truth is I'm going to get up on time because I want to be a person of integrity. I didn't come out here to sleep in. I want to get up and walk with Jesus Christ. I know He starts his day early and I want to be with Him so I'll get up on time."

Overcoming this personal weakness will make this missionary one who can boldly declare:

> "Mr. Johnson, you can overcome smoking. I know by personal experience that we can be stronger than our appetites and habits. The Lord wants you to do this. Giving up smoking, starting today, will change your entire life. I promise you in the name of the Lord that you will be blessed with the power to overcome this habit. Will you, from this moment on, forsake smoking?"

This missionary is now, in this matter, a man of integrity. From this foundation he can build a mission and a life of integrity.

From The Weakness Of Succumbing To Peer Pressure To The Strength Of Being Self-directed

In high school, a certain missionary had been influenced negatively by peer group pressure. He felt weak in his power to withstand the forces of such pressure.

As his mission begins he desires to overcome this weakness. He has an intense desire to do the right things. Soon some missionaries call him "gung ho." He feels they are ridiculing him. He decides to "lighten up."

One day, those in his district say, "Let's drive over there. There's a cave over there and we can go through it today on our preparation day."

He says, "Well, that's out of our district."

And they say, "So what?"

He says, "I don't think we should go there."

"We're going. Anyway, who's going to know about it?"

So they go and the missionary goes with them. All the while he feels guilty. The next time he goes along again. He feels weak and his spiritual confidence begins to wane as his compliance with mission rules become less and less.

He feels his mission will never end. He wishes it was over now. He is far less effective as a missionary than he dreamed that he would be. He prays fervently for help. He hears the enticings of the Holy Spirit. He decides to be his own master. He decides that if keeping the mission rules makes him unpopular with some, then so be it.

Thereafter when someone suggest something that is out-side the rules, he balks at their suggestions. They say, "No one will know."

He says with a smile, "I'll know about it, and I won't go."

They reply, "Well, we can't go without you."

And he says, "Why don't we all stay here and play a little softball?"

So they say, "Good idea."

The missionary now has greater strength. Now he feels inclined to be more meek and submissive and easy to be entreated by the leaders of the mission and by the Lord. He becomes more bold in teaching and challenging the people. He also becomes more bold in encouraging other missionaries to rise up above mediocrity. Overcoming his former weakness makes him a missionary with power and boldness.

He is learning what a joy it is to be obedient. Not because he has to, but because he wants to. Such an attitude will enable him to serve with joy on his mission and all his life.

From The Weakness Of Self-abuse To The Strength Of Moral Virtue

Some missionaries, in their adolescent years developed a habit of personal immorality. This habit of self-abuse becomes very difficult for them to overcome. They tried to rid them-selves of it prior to their mission, but then it returns as they serve. Their desire to be worthy causes them to feel that they must avoid this habit, yet, in a time of weakness, it happens. When it does all the joys of missionary work are lessened. Their spiritual sensitivities are deadened, and their confidence departs. They become timid and uncertain. The enticings of the Holy Spirit seem silenced.

This awful habit can be overcome. But to do so requires a marshalling of all the forces that can be mustered.

I now write boldly to a missionary who has this problem:

Dear Missionary,

No one needs to add to your feelings of guilt. You already have such feelings. Remember, guilt is a great motivator when coupled with a positive plan for recovery. Pray to Heavenly Father for His help. Tell Him of your desire to overcome this weakness. He will bless you with a strength far beyond your own.

Talk to your mission president and to no one else about this problem. Your president will not punish you. He will encourage you. He will serve as someone to whom you can report regarding your goals to overcome this habit. Try to go longer each time between the occurrences. If you fall back, contact your president and renew your efforts.

Do positive things. Get up on time. Stay with your companion. Avoid being alone in the places where the problem occurs. You know the feelings that precede this indiscretion. Read the scriptures, look at pictures of your family and of the Savior.

Be bold in prayer and in proclaiming to yourself that you know you can win this battle—it is a battle—a battle that can and will be won. A battle that when won, will forever enable you to be a bold missionary. A missionary who can promise others, in the name of the

Lord, that they can win their battles. Overcoming this weakness will give you a foundation of strength that will enable you to live a life of chastity, virtue and spiritual power.

In this and in all matters of weakness your personal efforts, coupled with prayer, are your main source of strength. Your mission president can be your partner in assisting and encouraging you. He is the Lord's agent and his stewardship includes your physical and spiritual welfare. He will receive inspiration from the Lord on how to best assist you. Turn to him. Trust him. Make him your partner and spiritual confidant. He can only help if you allow him to do so.

Jesus Christ is not a future Savior to you. He is your Savior now—everyday. Through His grace we can gain the strength to change inward lust to heartfelt virtue. That is the message we teach. When you experience that power, then and only then will you be able to boldly promise others that they can change their lives.

From Weakness Of Deception
To Strength Of Integrity

Missionaries can cease from any desire to deceive. Some, just a few, are a bit deceptive. They try to get a way with stuff. It saddens me to write what I just wrote. I would edit it out, except it is true. Such missionaries make up false reports and in their interviews, they don't tell the truth. They're trying to see what they can get away with. Such Elders could never speak boldly of trusting God, for they know that they are not trustworthy. The main requirement to make this change is a decision to be honest in all your dealings with yourself and your fellowmen. Perhaps this is the easiest weakness to overcome, but the rewards of doing so will be everlasting as the missionary's greatest strength will be his integrity.

From The Weakness Of Being Too Boisterous To The Strength Of Balancing Exuberance And Dignity

A missionary can change from being a loud mouth, to being sort of a quiet guy. They don't have to change completely, because often, they are charming and their personality is good for the morale of others. Yet some are just a little bit too loud, a little too boisterous. They can change by turning down the volume of their spoken words and their laughter. They can add a flavor of dignity to their exuberance.

From The Weakness Of Being Self-centered To The Strength Of Being Others-Centered

Some missionaries love to be center stage. Quite often, it's really nice for them to step off center stage and push their companion out there. Figuratively speaking, tell him, "Get out there Elder and take a bow." If he is one of those who doesn't ever want to be in the spotlight—one who kind of wants to hide— then boldly encourage him, in the name of Jesus Christ, to get out there and take center stage . Tell him that you know he can do it. In meetings praise him. In teaching always say, "My companion and I," instead of, "I." Use the word, "We" instead of "I."

One of the chief characteristics of a bold missionary is that he always has a great companion. He considers it his primary responsibility to make his companion great. To do this, be generous in complimenting him for the good that he does.

Both the extraverted and the introverted missionaries can change, and yet they can still be their old self. When they go back to Delta, Utah or Ely, Nevada, people will still know who they are. They will be the same and yet they will be different. The loud fellow will still have that gregarious personality, however there will be a beautiful balance of exuberance and dignity. From such a foundation the missionary will be bold in influencing others for good.

The quiet, more timid departing missionary will still be quite reserved upon coming home. However his quiet nature will be tempered with a boldness that amazes those who engage him in private conversation, or who hear him speak and teach. His former weakness which gave the impression of humility, will now through his faith in Christ, be true humility with the resulting power.

From The Weakness Of Seeing And Acting Negatively To The Power Of Seeing And Being Part Of The Good

Some missionaries specialize in the weakness of sarcasm and negative thinking. They think everything is wrong. They are cynical and they make light of those who strive to do the right things. They see the dark side of everybody and of every situation. Never have I met such a missionary who had the Spirit. Such thinking blocks out the Spirit of the Lord.

Such missionaries think they are clever and fascinating when engaged in sarcastic gossip. Some other missionaries like to talk to them to hear and be amused by the latest dirt. Be careful in your association with such disgruntled ones. It is easier to tear down than to build. Negative missionaries are never spiritually bold, and they can strip boldness from others.

Such missionaries can change. Often they are intelligent and insightful. They realize the price they are paying for the supposed luxury of being a chief and clever critic. Hopefully they will "come to themselves." Then they will know that their time to change has come. Through their prayers and their inward sense of what is right they will be prompted to change. They will decide to use their skills to build their companions, the mission rules, the missionary leaders, and the mission president. They will, in the name of Jesus Christ and through His power, listen to the enticings of the Holy Spirit. They will make this former and devastating weakness into a force for good that will help change the morale and spirituality of the entire mission.

From Weakness Of Being Timid
To The Strength Of Being Bold

One of the changes that was really difficult for me was changing from being timid to being confident.

We could say that this change is the big one—the most essential one. However, this change will be the by-product of all the other changes that we make.

Some of us, because of our past, have a long way to go to make this change. Consider this story from my pre-mission days.

Once on kind of a self-dare, I asked the girl of my dreams to go to the movie with me. I was shocked when she accepted. I walked fearfully to her house and the two of us walked silently to the theater. As we entered I stopped and bought a bag of popcorn. As we watched the movie, I began to eat the popcorn. I knew that I should offer her some, but I was fearful to do so. What would I do if she told me no? I could not stand such rejection. So, out of fear, I ate the whole bag myself.

I know that this story sounds ridiculous, but it is true not only of me, but also of others. Some missionaries, because of fear, are unwilling to ask a person on a bus or at the bank if they know anything about the Church. They are fearful to challenge the people they meet to allow them to come in to their home and teach them. They hesitate to challenge people they are teaching to come to church or to give up smoking for fear of offending them or of being rejected by them. They, because of fear, do not share, but eat the whole bag of popcorn them-selves.

Some of us don't feel like we could ever be a really bold mis-sionary. We just don't think it's in us. We rationalize and say, "I just can't be pushy." It scares us to think about being bold.

The most common enemy to making a change is fear. We're fearful that if we try new things we will look bad in the eyes of others. We are afraid that a big, bearded guy will come to the door while we're tracting and when he does we retreat without giving him a fair shot. We'd sooner talk to little ladies than big tough looking guys. We're afraid that people will think it's strange if we start talking to them on a street corner, or in a bus when they don't even know us. We fear that if we're really obedient to the mission rules, the other missionaries will think that we are an apple polisher, or something like that. We're really afraid of the opinions we feel the other missionaries have of us. Most of all, we are just sort of afraid of ourselves.

Few missionaries are completely bold or completely fearful. So this is an area of change that we all need to make.

In the Doctrine and Covenants, the Lord said to one group of missionaries,

> "But with some I am not well pleased, for they will not open their mouths, (I wonder why they wouldn't open their mouths?) but they hide the talent which I have given unto them." *(D&C 60:2)*

Why?

The Lord says it is:

> "...because of the fear of man. Wo unto such, for mine anger is kindled against them. And it shall come to pass, if they are not more faithful unto me, it shall be taken away, even that which they have." *(D&C 60:2)*

"Because of the fear of man." Those words rank as the saddest words that could ever be said of a missionary. How would you like it if your mission president, in your final release letter, to your folks, wrote, "Your son is coming home. He would have been a great missionary except for his fear of man."

Early in this book I related the sad story of how fear caused me to be weak in presenting the gospel message to a philosophy professor. When my companion, Elder Blair, told me that I had been wishy washy, I felt awful. I resolved to forever do better. Since then, I have constantly tried, in humility and with faith, to present the gospel principles as facts.

Presenting the gospel principles as facts, received within your soul from the Holy Ghost, invites the Holy Ghost to witness to those we teach that our words are true. We say, "God answers prayers." The Holy Ghost says inside of their souls, "That is true."

In order to boldly testify to the Lord's words, and to teach the gospel principles as facts, we must constantly yield to the enticings of the Holy Spirit. We must be easy to be entreated. We must constantly seek virtue. Then with solemnity of heart and the spirit of meekness, we can speak boldly, in the name of Jesus Christ.

What is the cure if we do feel some fear?

Mormon said:

"I speak with boldness, having authority from God,
I fear not what man can do; for perfect love casteth out
all fear." *(Moroni 8:16)*

Therefore the answers seems to be, if we feel timid and fearful when we're walking up to a door, we should not pray that we won't be afraid and that we'll feel bold. Rather we should pray somewhat like this:

52

"Heavenly Father I'm going up on that porch. Help me to love the people who come to the door. Help me to love them with a perfect love."

Then, just as the Lord has promised, all our fears will be cast out and through the Holy Spirit, we will be bold. Why? Because perfect love casteth out all fear.

It is not as if we can say that on February 6, 2002, I quit being timid and haven't been timid since. The battle between timid and bold must be waged each day and each hour. When we feel a bit weak and timid, we usually need to repent and to change some weakness into a strength. We need to pray aloud and silently for love and for good feelings. Then we will feel the power come back into us which will enable us to be sweetly bold.

We must not do less than we should because of the fear of man. We must open our mouths, so the Lord will be pleased with us, but more than that, so that people will have the opportunity to hear and know the truth.

8

A LITTLE CHANGE CAN BRING
A MIGHTY CHANGE IN BOLDNESS

Probably none of the weaknesses we just discussed are your weaknesses. Yet it is a certainty that you have your own personal weaknesses. As you serve the Lord, the degree of boldness you will have in asking others to make changes, will be directly proportional to the dedication that you have to making your weaknesses into strengths.

Even to make a little change is difficult, let alone a mighty change such as the one that the scriptures tell us we ought to make. Always remember that a little change really is a mighty change.

Let me illustrate this:

Picture me facing toward you. Now watch me carefully. I turn just a slight degree or two, and now as I begin to walk forward, the further I go, the more I am away from where I would have been if I had kept going the direction I was faced before. You get the picture, don't you? So a meager little change now, can soon become an absolute mighty change—the mighty change that the Lord wants us to make. It is in making these small, but mighty changes that we receive the strength that makes us bold in speaking for Jesus Christ in inviting others to change.

Small changes such as being little less negative, being more helpful to your companion, expressing love and appreciation more often, praying a bit more specifically and with a little more faith. All these little change will be mighty changes.

9

ONCE YOU HAVE FOUND YOUR BOLDNESS, NEVER LET IT GO

Sometimes at the beginning of your mission, you may think that your time there will never end. However all to quickly, it will. Almost suddenly, it will be time for you to return home. Because you will yield to the enticings of the Holy Spirit and will be easy to be entreated, the time will fly by. Because you will change your weaknesses into strengths, the time will seem all too short. Because you will teach boldly, in the name of Jesus Christ, you will wonder why the time of your mission is passing so quickly.

When the end approaches, the thoughts of going home will not be what you, in the earlier days, had imagined. In your final interview with your mission president, you will likely say to him:

> "President, why didn't you let me go home when I first came? That is when I longed to be home. Now after all this time here, I feel I can't leave. The people here are my friends. They need me. The people I have taught depend on me. The younger missionaries seek my advice and my support. I can't desert them. I feel if I leave this whole mission might collapse."

Your mission president will smile a warm and understanding smile, and say:

"When I consider you going home, I too think this mission might collapse. The people and the other missionaries will miss you. Your bold teaching has influenced every one of them."

He then adds with emotion:

"Most of all, I will miss you. I have always known that when I didn't know where to turn to help a troubled missionary, I could always turn to you."

He might well read you the words which the Lord spoke to Nephi:

"Blessed art thou... (Elder), for those things which thou hast done; for I have beheld how thou hast with unwearyingness declared the word, which I have given unto thee, unto this people. And thou has not feared them, and has not sought thine own life, but hast sought my will, and to keep my commandments.

"And now, because thou has done this,... I will bless thee forever; and I will make thee mighty in word and deed, in faith and in works..." *(Helaman 10:4-5)*

Your president continues:

"You've worked with unwearyingness. You haven't

been afraid. You've spoken boldly. You've not sought your own will, but the Lord's. You've yielded your will to His, not because you had to, but because you wanted to."

Then the president says,

"Now it is time for you to go home. You'll soon find a young woman. You will love her, and she will love you. You will boldly ask her to marry you. The two of you will be blessed forever because you will continue to be bold in your spiritual life and in teaching your children."

Final Note From Me To You

The seeds of boldness are within you. If you do not resist the enticings of the Holy Spirit these seeds will grow and you will be the means of doing much good. The message of the Lord will come through you to many others. Their entire eternity will be altered because you were bold in teaching them the truth. Your mission will be glorious and the blessings of the Lord will flow unto you forever.

ABOUT THE AUTHOR

George D. Durrant was born and raised in American Fork, Utah. He has served in many capacities with the LDS Church Educational System. For several years he was the director of Priesthood Genealogy for the church.

He served for three years as president of the Missionary Training Center in Provo, Utah, and he has taught religion at Brigham Young University.

He is the author of more than a dozen books, including the best-selling *Scones for the Heart, Love at Home—Starring Father* and *Don't Forget the Star*.

He is married to the former Marilyn Burnham. They are the parents of eight children.

Other Cedar Fort books
by George Durrant

Scones for the Heart

One of George Durrant's favorite memories is the day his mother cooked a batch of warm, delicious scones—just for him. We each carry "scones" of a different sort in our hearts. There are scones of kind words and generous deeds. This uplifting collection of 184 stories shares "scones" that will warm your soul and sweeten your life.

Don't Forget the Star

This book is filled with yuletide memories that humorously yet tenderly show how we love Christmas as youngsters, lose focus as teenagers, then rediscover its true meaning later in life. A holiday classic the whole family will love.

Find these books at your local bookstore
*or order them at **www.cedarfort.com***

9 26575 76739 4